W9-DIB-483

Livonia Public Library
ALFRED NOBLE
32901 PLYMOUTH ROAD
Livonia, Michigan 48150-1793
421-6600
LIVN #D

J932
M

EGYPTIAN
MUMMIES

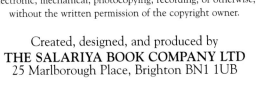

Author:

Henrietta McCall studied Egyptology at Oxford University in England. She is the author of **Pyramids** in the *Fast Forward* series and **Mesopotamian Myths**. Henrietta has also edited numerous children's books on ancient Egypt and is a member of the Council of the British Museum Society.

Artist:

Dave Antram was born in Brighton, England, in 1958. He studied at Eastbourne College of Art and then worked in advertising for 15 years before becoming a full-time artist. He has illustrated many children's non-fiction books.

Series creator:

David Salariya was born in Dundee, Scotland. In 1989 he established The Salariya Book Company. He has illustrated a wide range of books and has created many new series for publishers in the UK and overseas. He lives in Brighton with his wife, the illustrator Shirley Willis, and their son.

Editor:

Karen Barker Smith

Additional artists:

Mark Bergin
John James
Carolyn Scrace

© The Salariya Book Company Ltd MM
All rights reserved. No part of this book may be reproduced, stored in a retrieval system, or transmitted in any form or by any means, electronic, mechanical, photocopying, recording, or otherwise, without the written permission of the copyright owner.

Created, designed, and produced by
THE SALARIYA BOOK COMPANY LTD
25 Marlborough Place, Brighton BN1 1UB

ISBN 0-531-11877-0 (Lib. Bdg.)
ISBN 0-531-16443-8 (Pbk.)

Published in America by Franklin Watts
Grolier Publishing Co., Inc.
Sherman Turnpike, Danbury, CT 06816

Visit Franklin Watts on the
internet at: http://publishing.grolier.com

A CIP catalog record for this title is available
from the Library of Congress.

Repro by Modern Age.

Printed in China

3 9082 08593 7194

OCT 1 0 2001

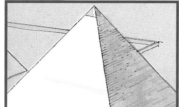

EGYPTIAN MUMMIES

Written by
HENRIETTA McCALL

Illustrated by
DAVE ANTRAM

Created and designed by
DAVID SALARIYA

W
FRANKLIN WATTS
A Division of Grolier Publishing
NEW YORK • LONDON • HONG KONG • SYDNEY
DANBURY, CONNECTICUT

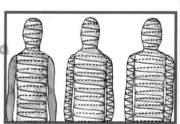

Livonia Public Library
ALFRED NOBLE BRANCH
32901 PLYMOUTH ROAD
Livonia, Michigan 48150-1793
421-6600
LIVN #19

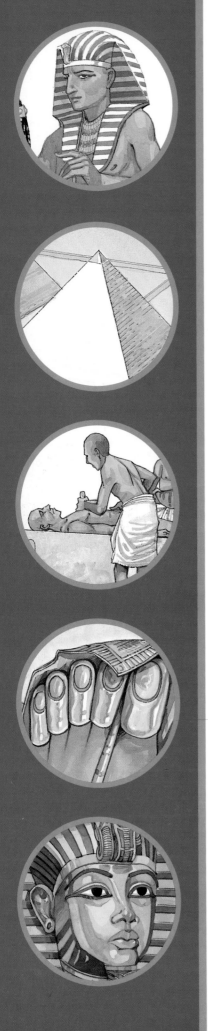

Contents

Ancient Egypt

The ancient land of Egypt was divided into two parts: the Black Land and the Red Land. The Black Land, which the Egyptians called *kemet*, was the fertile land all along the banks of the River Nile. The land was fertile because of the great flood (called the Inundation), which took place every year between July and September. At this time, the river rose higher and higher until it burst its banks and flooded all the nearby countryside with rich, muddy water that turned the land black. Farmers could then sow wheat, barley, and vegetables for the coming year. Occasionally, the river did not flood the land, and when this happened many animals and people died of starvation. The Red Land, called *deshret*, consisted of vast areas where nothing would grow. This was where stone was quarried for great temples and tombs and turquoise, malachite, and gold were mined.

Shu was the god of light. His son, Geb, was the god of earth, and Shu's daughter, Nut, was goddess of the sky. The ancient Egyptians believed that Nut swallowed the sun at nightfall, that it traveled through her body during the night hours, and at dawn she gave birth to it once more. Nut is often pictured in an arched position, as if she is the sky arched over the flat form of the earth (above).

Each king (also known as a pharaoh) of ancient Egypt usually had many wives, but the most important was called the Chief Royal Wife. She was often the mother of the future king, but may have been the one the king loved the most. The mother of the present king was also an important figure in the royal palace, as she had given life to the king.

Chief Royal Wife

Pharaoh

7

Death and Burial

Some people think that the ancient Egyptians were obsessed with death. In fact, the opposite is true. They so much enjoyed their lives in the well-ordered, rich, and beautiful land of Egypt that they wanted to live forever. As that was not possible, they wanted their next life, or afterlife, to be just as good as, if not better than, life on earth.

The ancient Egyptians believed that every human had two spiritual parts: the *ba*, which was responsible for a person's character, and the *ka*, which represented a person's life force. When someone died, his *ka* was believed to live on in his physical body, so it was essential to preserve it. This was achieved by a complicated process called mummification.

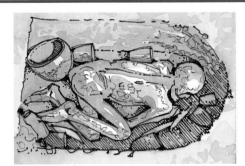

Only rich people were mummified. Poor people were buried in pits dug in the sand, and because Egypt is so dry and hot, their bodies were often naturally mummified. The bodily fluids leaked into the hot sand, the body dried out, and the skin covering the skeleton became hard and leathery. Objects such as pots or beads were often left beside the body.

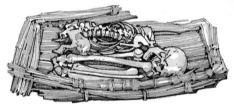

Every Egyptian settlement had its own cemetery, or city of the dead, which Egyptologists call a necropolis. Private citizens were buried there, often with gold jewelry, weapons, or finely decorated pottery. Above, a reed coffin.

The low rectangular structure of a mastaba tomb was built of mud brick or stone above an underground chamber. Often the walls of the burial chamber were decorated with scenes of daily life, and the dead person was buried with goods for the afterlife.

Step Pyramid   *Bent Pyramid*

Egyptian kings were buried in pyramids. The earliest known pyramid is the Step Pyramid at Saqqara (above left). It had six "steps," each one smaller than the one below it. It was the burial place of King Djoser about 2611 B.C. About 60 years later, the Egyptians learned how to build true pyramids, by using packing blocks to fill in the "steps." Occasionally things went wrong. When the Bent Pyramid (above right) was half built, the architects decided to change the angle so that the top half is much more steeply inclined than the bottom.

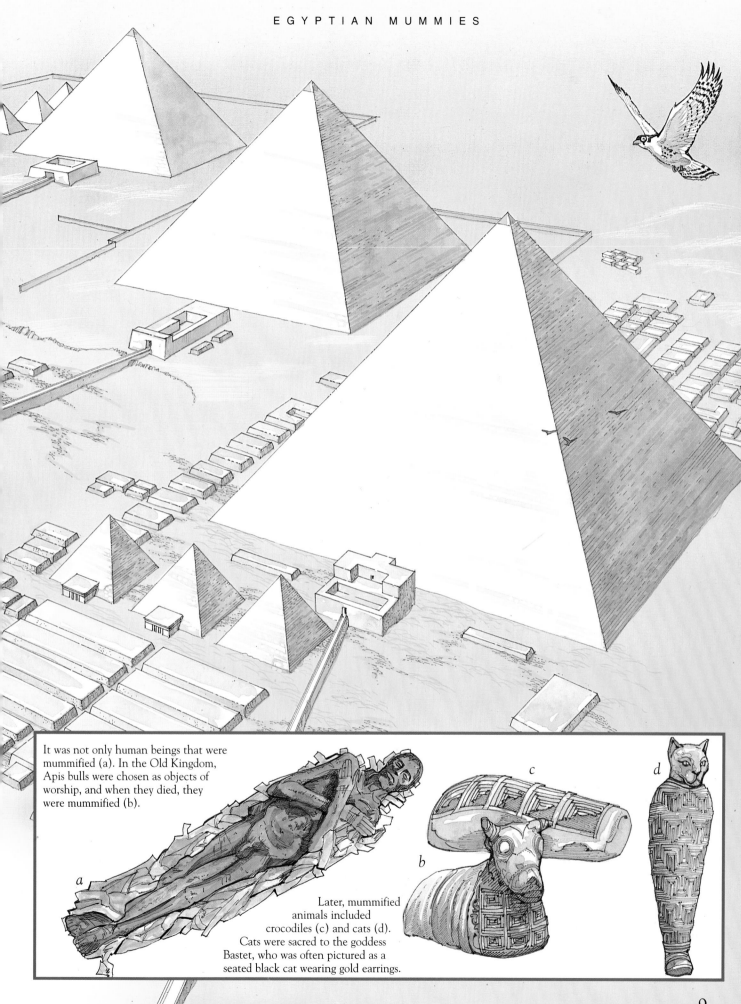

It was not only human beings that were mummified (a). In the Old Kingdom, Apis bulls were chosen as objects of worship, and when they died, they were mummified (b).

Later, mummified animals included crocodiles (c) and cats (d). Cats were sacred to the goddess Bastet, who was often pictured as a seated black cat wearing gold earrings.

Preparing the Mummy

Egypt is a very hot country, so when a person died, his or her body was taken away at once, to be mummified. It took 70 days to complete the whole process. First, the brain was removed through the nostrils with an iron hook. Then a cut was made in the abdomen through which all the internal organs were removed, including the lungs, stomach, and intestines. The body was then thoroughly washed with palm wine followed by water mixed with ground spices. When it was as clean as possible, the inside was filled with sweet-smelling herbs and spices and the cut sewn up.

The body was dried out in a bath of natron, a form of salt. After 40 days, the skin looked like leather. It was then oiled and stuffed where necessary to make it look lifelike and wrapped from head to foot in strips of linen bandages. Amulets were placed in particular positions inside the bandages, and, finally, a mask was put over the head.

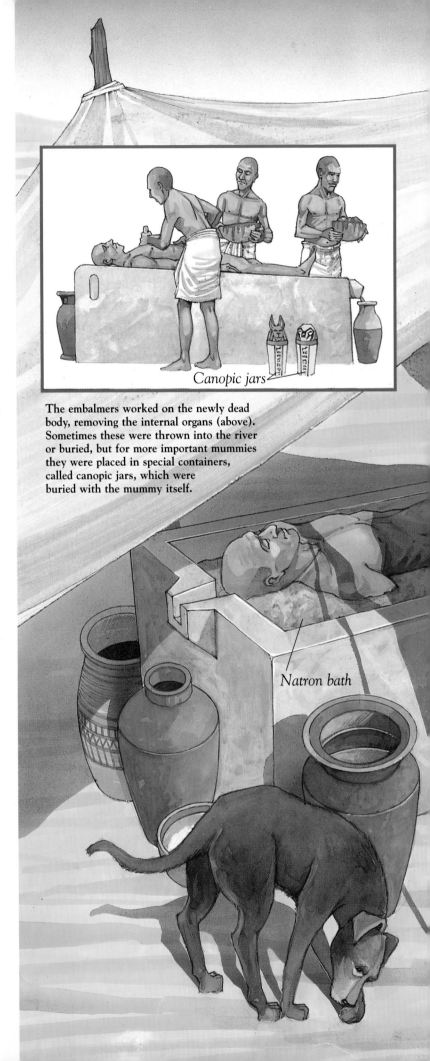

Canopic jars

The embalmers worked on the newly dead body, removing the internal organs (above). Sometimes these were thrown into the river or buried, but for more important mummies they were placed in special containers, called canopic jars, which were buried with the mummy itself.

Natron bath

This copy of an ancient wall painting shows the priests washing the body and pouring water over the head (top). The body is then laid on a couch (bottom) while the priest, dressed as the jackal-headed god of the underworld, Anubis, reads out magic spells.

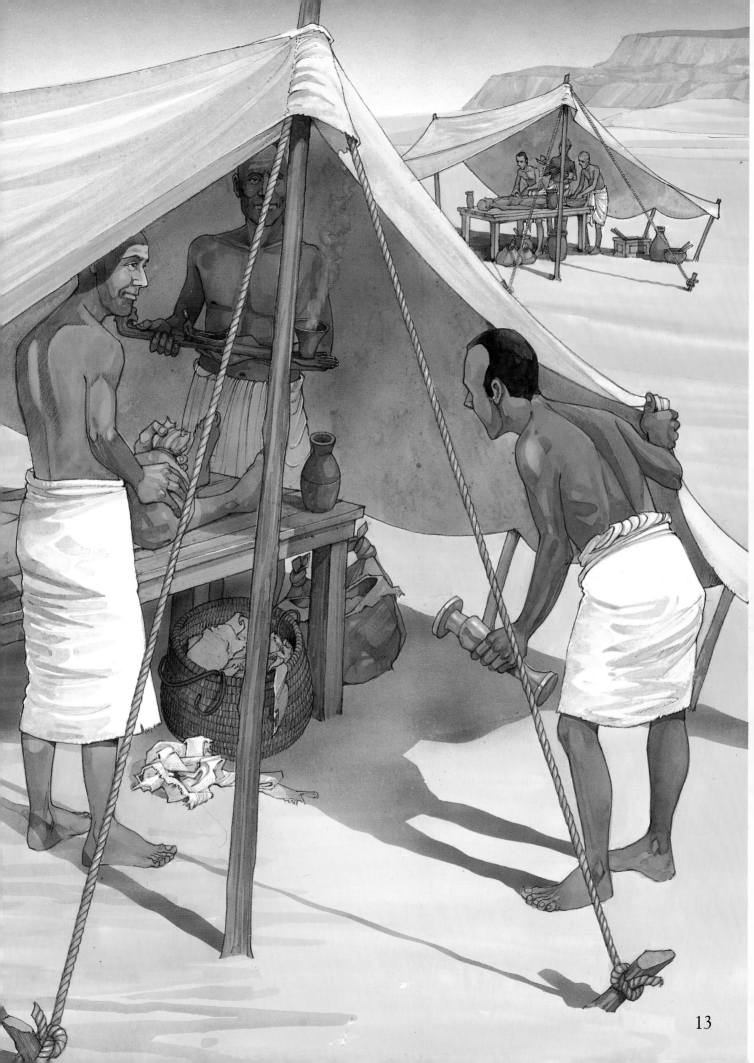

Wrapping the Mummy

Once the embalmers had done their work on the body, it was time for priests to wrap it in linen. Flax, from which linen is made, was grown throughout Egypt's history. However, linen was an expensive material, and some mummies were wrapped in recycled linen strips: Quite often garments the deceased had worn in life were torn up to provide their mummy wrappings. In later periods, special linen sheets were woven and then torn into strips.

As the wrapping process progressed, priests chanted spells. Some later mummies had spells written directly on to the wrappings themselves. Amulets were carefully inserted in specially designated places as protection devices and to ward off evil spirits.

For more elaborate mummies, the fingers and toes were individually wrapped. Egyptologists know from the mummy of King Tutankhamun that royal fingers and toes had special gold covers pushed over them. The covers, called finger or toe stalls, had the fingernails and toenails beautifully drawn on them. Tutankhamun's mummy also wore golden sandals with curled toes and a thong that ran between the big toe and the next.

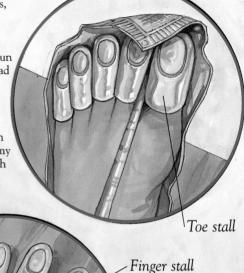

Toe stall

Finger stall

Liquid resin

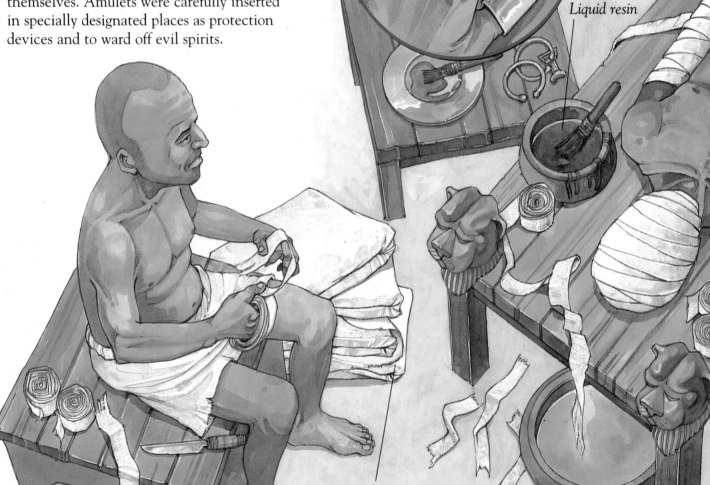

Linen for mummy wrapping

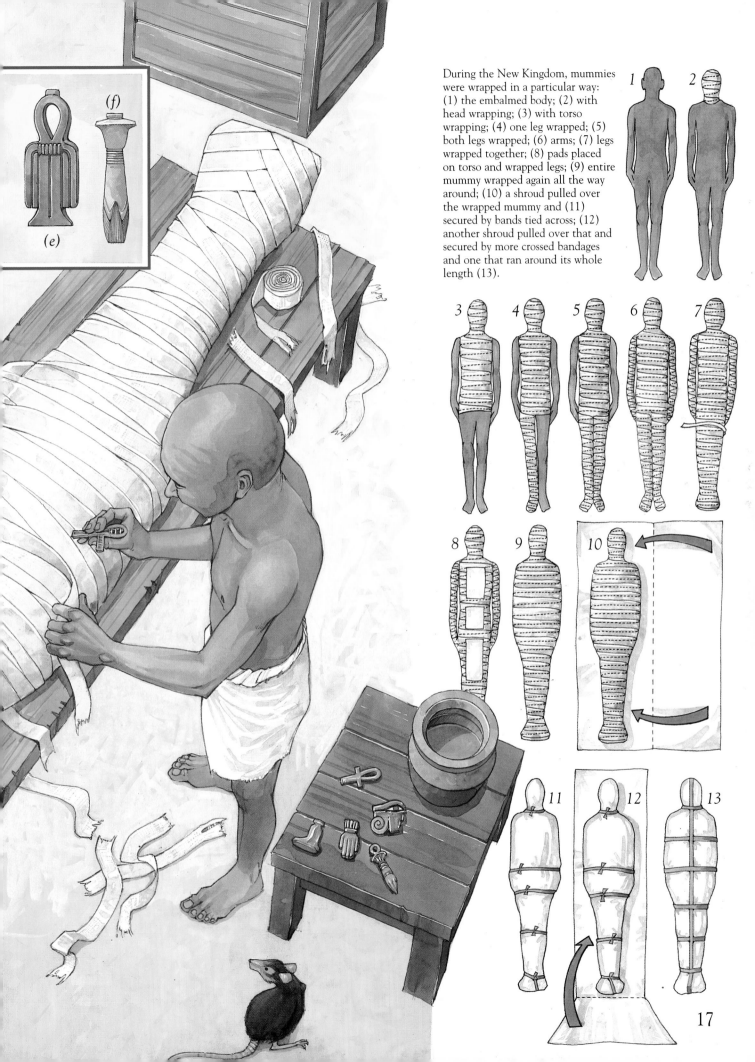

During the New Kingdom, mummies were wrapped in a particular way: (1) the embalmed body; (2) with head wrapping; (3) with torso wrapping; (4) one leg wrapped; (5) both legs wrapped; (6) arms; (7) legs wrapped together; (8) pads placed on torso and wrapped legs; (9) entire mummy wrapped again all the way around; (10) a shroud pulled over the wrapped mummy and (11) secured by bands tied across; (12) another shroud pulled over that and secured by more crossed bandages and one that ran around its whole length (13).

(e)

(f)

1
2
3
4
5
6
7
8
9
10
11
12
13

17

Mummy Cases and Coffins

In the Old Kingdom, coffins were usually rectangular wooden boxes with a single line of painted text asking for food in the afterlife. Sometimes they were painted with a pair of eyes so that the mummy could "see" out.

Later coffins were more brightly painted, with spells on the inside and more decoration outside. Rectangular coffins were more or less abandoned in favor of anthropoid coffins — wooden boxes in the shape of a human body. These coffins could be very elaborate indeed and highly colored. In simple burials, the mummy was placed in one anthropoid coffin within a large stone chest, called a sarcophagus. Royal burials involved a number of decorated anthropoid coffins, each fitting neatly into the next, and all placed in a sarcophagus.

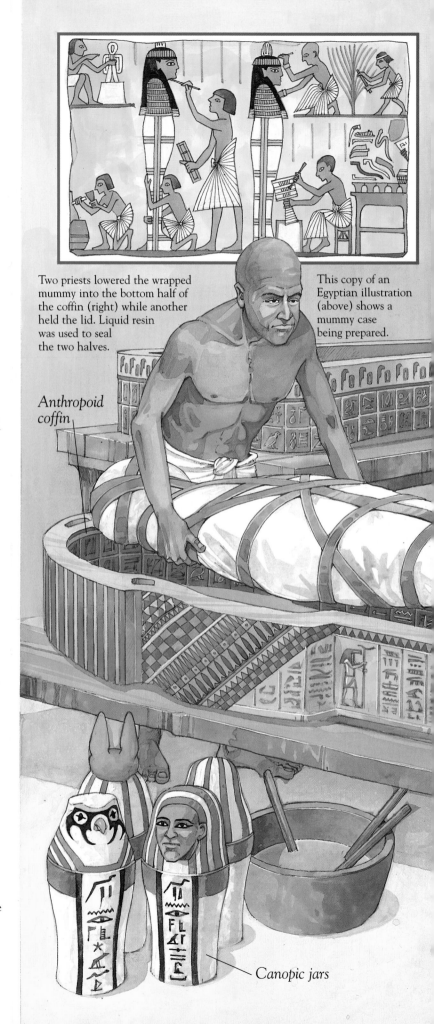

Two priests lowered the wrapped mummy into the bottom half of the coffin (right) while another held the lid. Liquid resin was used to seal the two halves.

This copy of an Egyptian illustration (above) shows a mummy case being prepared.

Anthropoid coffin

Canopic jars

This golden mask of the boy king Tutankhamun (above) is thought to be an exact likeness of him. The mask was made from beaten gold, inlaid with precious stones and colored glass paste. On his forehead, the king wore the uraeus, representing the dual land of Upper and Lower Egypt. This and the false beard beneath his chin are symbols of kingship.

A priest dressed as Anubis (below) ensured that the amulets were all in place and that the mask was properly fitted over the bandaged face.

Anubis mask

Canopic chest

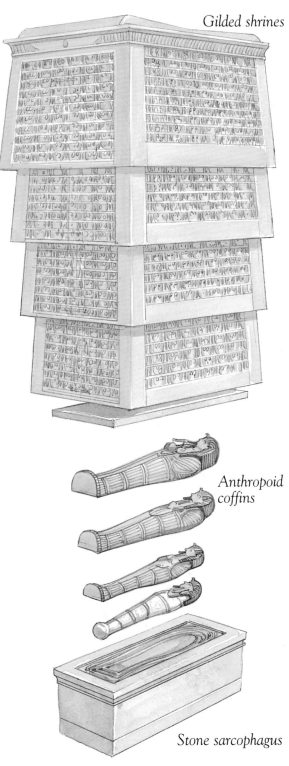

Gilded shrines

Anthropoid coffins

Stone sarcophagus

The more important the person, the more coffins he or she had. Egyptologists know from the tomb of Tutankhamun that even a boy king had three anthropoid coffins, one of which was solid gold. These were inside a stone sarcophagus, which in turn had been placed inside four shrines, each made of gilded wood and elaborately decorated.

21

The Funeral Procession

Once the mummy was placed in its coffin or coffins, it was ready to be transported to the place of burial, where the great stone sarcophagus was waiting. The tomb itself had to be ready and well prepared with everything the dead person might need in the afterlife: food and drink, clothes, furniture, jewels, chariots, and even servants. The "servants" were little pottery models called shabti figures, which the ancient Egyptians believed could stand in for the dead person's servants and do any hard work that might be required in the afterlife, such as cultivating crops for food. Some tombs contained hundreds of shabtis. They were usually glazed a brilliant blue and had a spell from the Book of the Dead inscribed on them so that they could answer the call to service.

The coffin was first placed in an open shrine on a papyrus boat (below). The boat was dragged on a sledge from the place of mummification to the dead person's home so that the family could accompany the deceased on his or her final journey. Then the boat was dragged down to the edge of the river. Burial sites were on the west bank of the Nile, as the west was considered sacred.

As the funeral procession approached the riverbank, more and more people would join it until quite a crowd had gathered. Friends and neighbors might carry some of the objects that were to stock the tomb (above).

Life expectancy was very short in ancient Egypt, and most people died long before middle age. Burials were a part of everyday life, and in larger villages and towns there were professional mourners — usually women — who joined the funeral procession (above). They wore blue to show they were mourning.

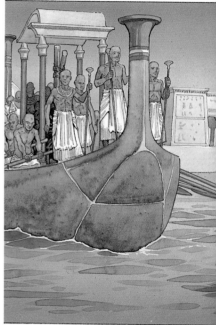

As the boat was rowed across the river (above), the mourners sang and wailed. When it reached the other side, the shrine was taken off, placed on a sledge, and dragged by oxen to the tomb. At the tomb the coffin was removed and placed upright against one of the walls inside. Priests then performed rituals in front of the coffin.

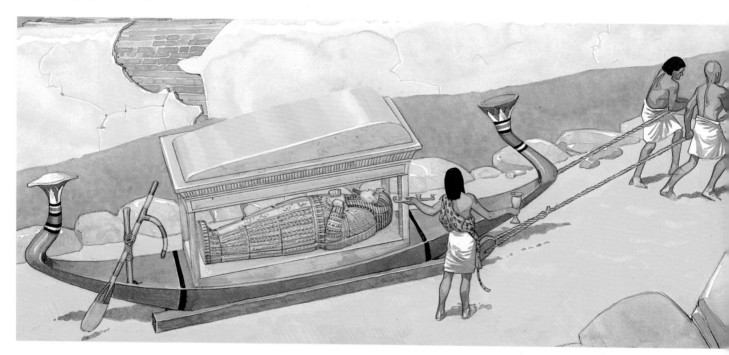

Opening-of-the-Mouth Ceremony

The most important ritual was the opening-of-the-mouth ceremony (right). To enable the dead person to eat and drink in the underworld, his mouth had to be "opened" by magic. It was also necessary to "open" his nose so he could breathe, his ears so he could hear, and his eyes so he could see. There were special instruments for doing this, usually types of flint knives, but sometimes the right leg bone of an ox was used. The ritual was usually performed by the eldest son and heir of the dead person.

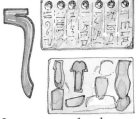

Instruments for the opening-of-the-mouth

Thoth

Anubis

Ammut

Ma'at

Feather of Truth

When the mummy reached the underworld, it had to undergo a final judgement before Osiris. The heart of the dead person was weighed against the feather of Ma'at, the goddess of truth (left). The dead person had to swear before 42 judges that he or she had done no wrong in life. Passing the test allowed them into the underworld, and they were declared "true of voice."

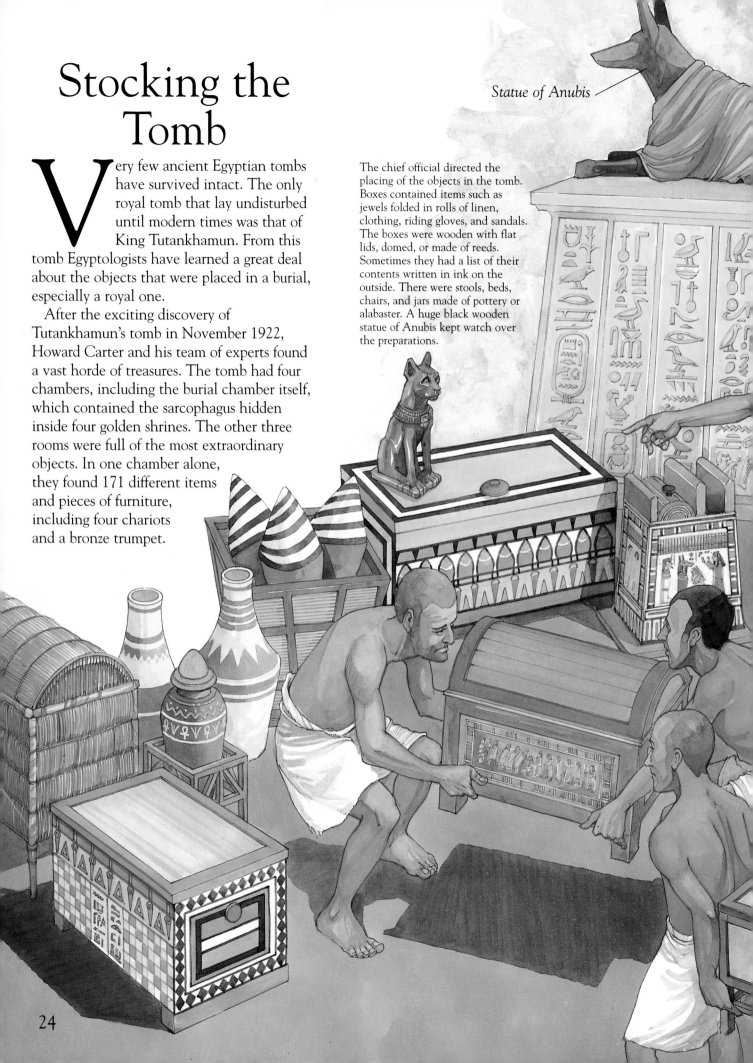

Stocking the Tomb

Very few ancient Egyptian tombs have survived intact. The only royal tomb that lay undisturbed until modern times was that of King Tutankhamun. From this tomb Egyptologists have learned a great deal about the objects that were placed in a burial, especially a royal one.

After the exciting discovery of Tutankhamun's tomb in November 1922, Howard Carter and his team of experts found a vast horde of treasures. The tomb had four chambers, including the burial chamber itself, which contained the sarcophagus hidden inside four golden shrines. The other three rooms were full of the most extraordinary objects. In one chamber alone, they found 171 different items and pieces of furniture, including four chariots and a bronze trumpet.

The chief official directed the placing of the objects in the tomb. Boxes contained items such as jewels folded in rolls of linen, clothing, riding gloves, and sandals. The boxes were wooden with flat lids, domed, or made of reeds. Sometimes they had a list of their contents written in ink on the outside. There were stools, beds, chairs, and jars made of pottery or alabaster. A huge black wooden statue of Anubis kept watch over the preparations.

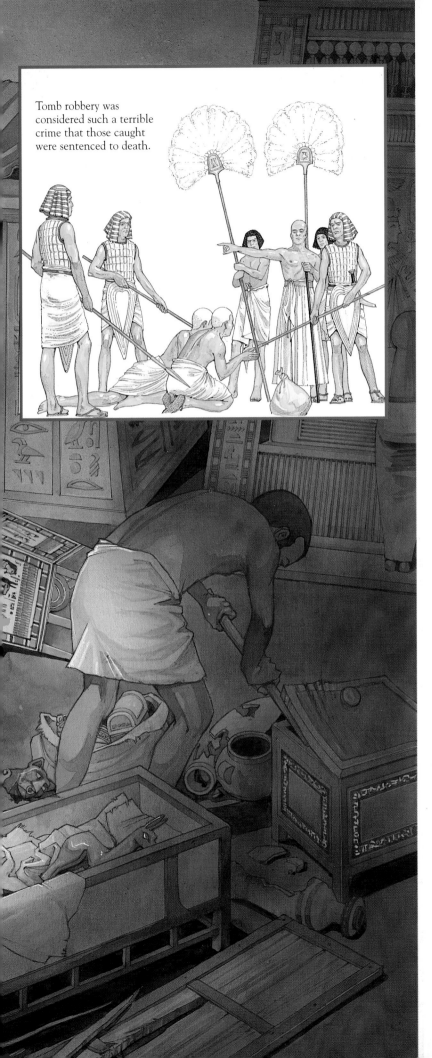

Tomb robbery was considered such a terrible crime that those caught were sentenced to death.

Shabtis were often placed all together in a special wooden chest (above). On the outside were recorded the name and titles of the dead person. It was thought that in the afterlife, the dead person only had to ask one of his shabtis to do a certain task and the shabti would reply, "I am here."

An offering table made of reeds held baskets of food (below). On the shelves were birds, and the baskets in front held flat loaves of bread and cakes made with honey and dates. Egypt's hot, dry climate has meant that these objects have survived thousands of years, though they have become very dry.

Boats were occasionally placed in burials (below), in case the mummy had to travel across water in the underworld. They were usually left unfinished, to fit inside the tomb, but every part would be there, ready to be put together.

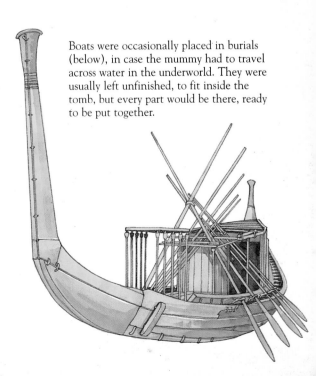

More Mummies

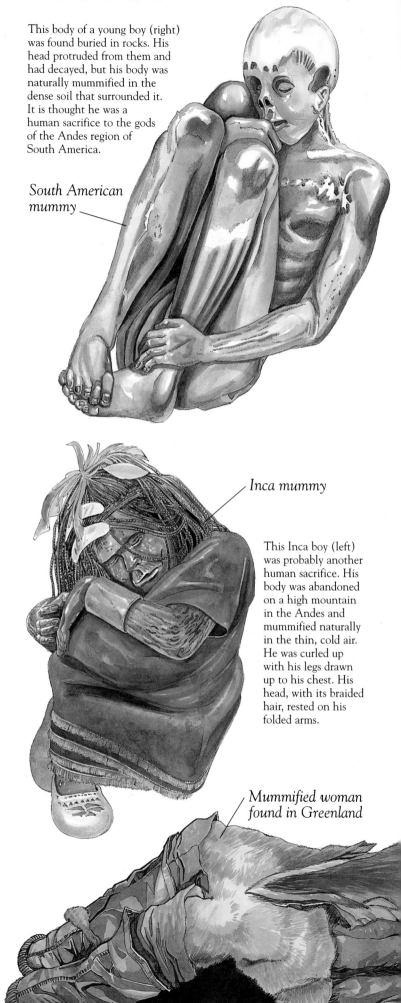

This body of a young boy (right) was found buried in rocks. His head protruded from them and had decayed, but his body was naturally mummified in the dense soil that surrounded it. It is thought he was a human sacrifice to the gods of the Andes region of South America.

South American mummy

The ancient Egyptians were not the only people who mummified their dead, though they were the first and the most skilled. About A.D. 200–600, the Nazca people of Peru also mummified their dead. The soft tissue was removed and the body packed with cotton and lime. The tendons of the legs and arms were cut so that the body could be neatly curled up. It was then dried out above glowing coals before being wrapped in cloth and put in a funerary pot.

Other bodies have been mummified naturally. In 1991, the body of a man was discovered in ice in an alpine pass, where it had lain for nearly 5,000 years. It is thought that he was a traveler who had been overcome by hunger and exhaustion and died. In Greenland, on the edge of the Arctic Circle, the bodies of six women, one 4-year-old child, and a baby were found in 1972. It was thought that the bodies had been mummified by the low temperatures and cold dry winds of the region.

An ill-fated Arctic expedition led by the British in the mid-nineteenth century ended in the entire team freezing to death. Their bodies were naturally mummified in the ice and snow.

Inca mummy

This Inca boy (left) was probably another human sacrifice. His body was abandoned on a high mountain in the Andes and mummified naturally in the thin, cold air. He was curled up with his legs drawn up to his chest. His head, with its braided hair, rested on his folded arms.

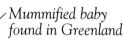
Mummified baby found in Greenland

The group of mummies found in Greenland date to about A.D. 1475. The mummified baby (left) is thought to be about six months old. He was fully clothed in sealskin. The skin of his face, as well as his hair and eyebrows, were preserved. One of the female mummies in the same grave was probably his mother. This female mummy (right) was probably only about 30 years old when she died judging by her hands, which showed little sign of wear.

Mummified woman found in Greenland

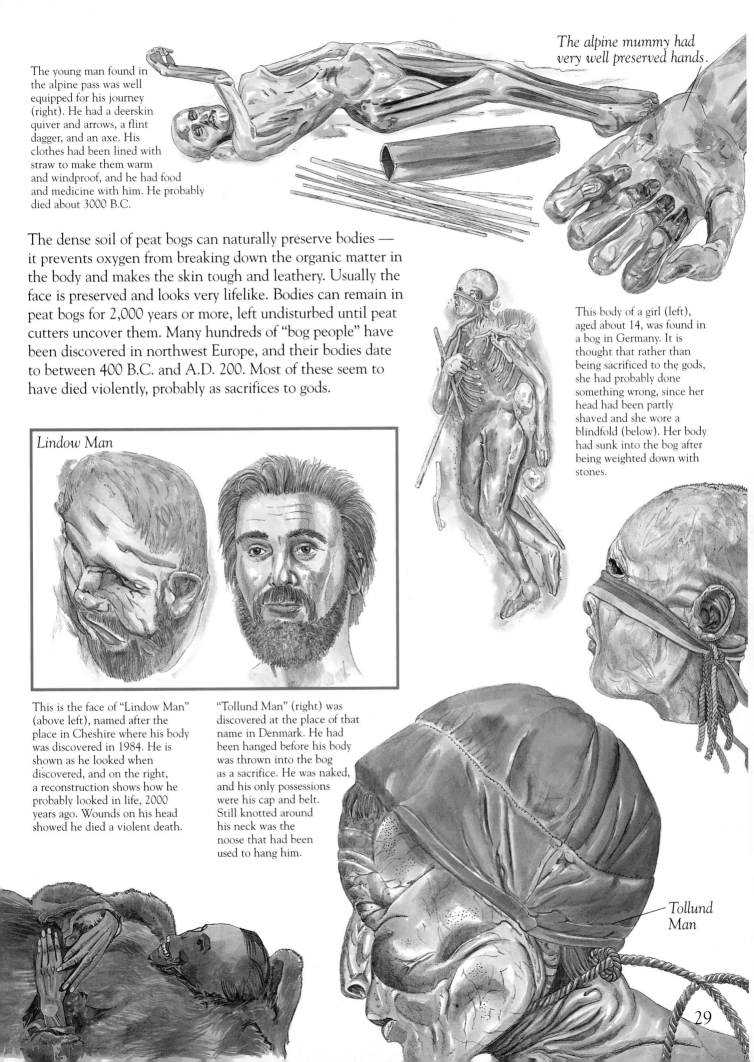

The young man found in the alpine pass was well equipped for his journey (right). He had a deerskin quiver and arrows, a flint dagger, and an axe. His clothes had been lined with straw to make them warm and windproof, and he had food and medicine with him. He probably died about 3000 B.C.

The alpine mummy had very well preserved hands.

The dense soil of peat bogs can naturally preserve bodies — it prevents oxygen from breaking down the organic matter in the body and makes the skin tough and leathery. Usually the face is preserved and looks very lifelike. Bodies can remain in peat bogs for 2,000 years or more, left undisturbed until peat cutters uncover them. Many hundreds of "bog people" have been discovered in northwest Europe, and their bodies date to between 400 B.C. and A.D. 200. Most of these seem to have died violently, probably as sacrifices to gods.

This body of a girl (left), aged about 14, was found in a bog in Germany. It is thought that rather than being sacrificed to the gods, she had probably done something wrong, since her head had been partly shaved and she wore a blindfold (below). Her body had sunk into the bog after being weighted down with stones.

Lindow Man

This is the face of "Lindow Man" (above left), named after the place in Cheshire where his body was discovered in 1984. He is shown as he looked when discovered, and on the right, a reconstruction shows how he probably looked in life, 2000 years ago. Wounds on his head showed he died a violent death.

"Tollund Man" (right) was discovered at the place of that name in Denmark. He had been hanged before his body was thrown into the bog as a sacrifice. He was naked, and his only possessions were his cap and belt. Still knotted around his neck was the noose that had been used to hang him.

Tollund Man

Glossary

Afterlife
The place where dead Egyptians arrived after passing through the underworld.

Ammut
A creature of the underworld with the head of a crocodile, the chest and front legs of a lioness, and the hindquarters of a hippopotamus.

Amulet
A small object like a lucky charm that was placed among the bandages of a mummy to ward off evil and keep the mummy safe on its way to the underworld.

Anthropoid coffins
Wooden boxes in the shape of a human body. They had two parts: the bottom half, in which the body was placed, and the lid, which was then sealed onto the base.

Anubis
The jackal-headed god of the underworld. The ancient Egyptians believed that he invented mummification.

Apis Bull
These were real bulls, chosen for their special markings (black and white with a diamond shape on their foreheads) that lived in palaces and were worshiped as gods. When an Apis bull died, he was mummified and buried in a special cemetery called the Serapeum.

Ba
The *ba* was believed to be the personality of a person. It was the duty of the *ba* to fly between the tomb and the underworld and to help the dead person reach the afterlife safely.

Book of the Dead
This was a series of spells, divided into 190 chapters. Some spells were recited during the mummification and funeral, while others were placed in the tomb to help the dead person in his or her journey to the afterlife.

Ka
The *ka* was a person's life force. When the person died, his *ka* lived on in his mummy.

Ma'at
The goddess of truth, justice, and order.

Malachite
A bright green stone used in ancient Egyptian jewelry or ground into powder and used as eye makeup.

Natron
A form of natural salt used for drying out a body during the mummification process.

Offerings
Many tombs contained a representation of a table of offerings so that the ka would have food in the afterlife. It was usually shown piled high with fowl, bread, vegetables, and fruit.

Old Kingdom, Middle Kingdom, and New Kingdom
The three main periods of Egyptian history when the pharaoh and the state were in full control. The Old Kingdom lasted from 2686–2181 B.C. and is also known as the Pyramid Age. Then came the First Intermediate Period (2181–2055 B.C.) — a time of unhappiness and chaos. The Middle Kingdom (2055–1650 B.C.) saw Egypt reunited into one country again, and art and literature flourished. The Second Intermediate Period (1650–1550 B.C.) was another time of disorder, when a foreign race called the Hyksos took over the north of the country. Egypt was reunited for the glorious period of the New Kingdom (1550–1069 B.C.) when it was the supreme world power.

Osiris
The god of the dead. He was murdered by his brother Seth, and Anubis made him into the first mummy. He is often symbolized by a djed-pillar, probably meant to represent his backbone.

Pottery plaque
A piece of baked clay painted to represent an eye and placed over the eye sockets of a mummy.

Professional mourners
These were usually women, hired to join an Egyptian funeral procession. They made a great deal of noise, loudly lamenting and wailing. They also threw their heads back and gave a gargling sound. This was called ululation and still occurs in Egypt today.

Resin
The sweet-smelling sap that oozes from fir and pine trees.

Sarcophagus (pl. Sarcophagii)
A large outer coffin, usually made of stone.

Shabtis
Pottery (and occasionally wood or stone) figurines in human shape buried with a mummy. Shabtis were called upon to do manual labor in the underworld for the dead person. Tutankhamun was buried with over 400 shabtis.

Thoth
The god of wisdom and writing. Sometimes he is shown as an ibis, sometimes as a baboon. He kept a record of how long a person was to live and what would happen to them.

Tyet-knot
A symbol sacred to the goddess Isis, representing a sandal strap.

Uraeus
A symbol worn on the forehead by the Egyptian king, both in life and death. It usually consisted of a cobra and a vulture and symbolized the power of the two goddesses who guarded Lower and Upper Egypt, Wadjyt and Nehkbet.

Mummies Facts

Tutankhamun was a boy king in the late New Kingdom. Egyptologists would know very little about him had it not been for the discovery of his nearly intact tomb by Howard Carter in 1922. Because his tomb contained such marvelous treasures, he became renowned throughout the world. During the 1920s and 1930s, there was a craze called Tutmania, which produced all sorts of things inspired by the discovery, for example, sewing machines, cigarettes, dances, and music.

In the months that followed the discovery of Tutankhamun's tomb in 1922, various people connected with the discovery died unusual deaths. Lord Carnarvon, who had paid for the search for the tomb, died suddenly of blood poisoning after being bitten on the cheek by a mosquito. Two others died: One was run over crossing the road and another fell out of a window. This gave rise to a belief in the "Curse of the Mummy." Egyptologists do not take the curse seriously, but it has been the source of much amusement and debate.

Spells that were painted on the inside of coffins are referred to as Coffin Texts by Egyptologists. They were there to help the dead person avoid danger and arrive safely in the afterlife.

The ancient Egyptian symbol for a person's *ba* was a bird with a human head and arms. The *ka* was shown as a pair of upraised arms.

During the 16th and 17th centuries A.D., ground mummy powder was considered a powerful drug, and people swallowed it for medicinal purposes. The ills it was supposed to cure ranged from sore throats and coughs to epilepsy and tuberculosis. Other people believed that if mummy powder was applied to a wound, the bleeding would stop. Because mummy powder was believed to be so powerful, many thousands of Egyptian mummies were broken up and ground down.

In Walt Disney's animated film *Snow White and the Seven Dwarfs*, mummy powder is used by the wicked stepmother in one of her evil spells.

There was a paint called Mummy Brown used in the 19th century for oil painting. This was actually made from little bits of mummies. One artist who discovered this was so horrified that he took his tubes of Mummy Brown out into the garden and gave them a proper burial! There is still a color called mummy brown.

The ancient Egyptians called the huge area of barren land in their country *deshret*, meaning red land. This is the source of our word "desert."

Over a period of 3,000 years, the exact way in which an ancient Egyptian mummy was bandaged changed. Sometimes the linen strips were wide, sometimes narrow. One woman was found wrapped in 16 layers of bandages, and a man mummified during the Middle Kingdom was wrapped in no less than 4,037 square feet (375 square meters) of linen.

Some ancient Egyptians grew so fond of their pets that when the animals died, they had them mummified and asked that they be placed in their tombs when they themselves died. Mummified gazelles, monkeys, dogs, and baboons have been found in tombs.

One tomb owner was so fond of his pet dog that he asked for its linen-wrapped mummy to be put at his feet in his coffin.

All mummies had their hearts weighed against the feather of truth before they could enter the underworld. This ritual is described in Chapter 125 of the Book of the Dead and was often illustrated on papyrus scrolls buried with the dead person. There is no record of anyone failing the test, but the underworld demon Ammut was sometimes shown waiting by the weighing scales to devour the heart of anyone whose evil deeds betrayed them. Without a heart, the dead person could not survive in the afterlife.

Thousands of sacred cats inhabited temples dedicated to the Egyptian cat goddess Bastet. They were mummified and buried when they died, and a huge number of cat mummies remain to this day.

Masks have always played an important part in the decoration of mummies. The earliest mummy masks found in Peru date to around 1200 B.C. and were made of red or brown cloth, which was stitched to the mummy dressing. In later periods burial masks were made of hammered sheet gold or copper with separate noses and teeth soldered on.

The ancient Incas mummified bodies by first filling them with tar and then exposing them alternately to severe frost at night and to the heat of the sun by day, until they were dried out completely. Then the body was placed in a niche or cave, where it did not rest undisturbed, but was frequently taken out for festivities, such as the celebration of military victories. The mummy would be taken to the place of celebration, dressed in sumptuous garments, seated on a golden chair, and given food and drink while people danced before it.

Index

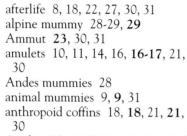

Illustrations are shown in **bold** type.

A
afterlife 8, 18, 22, 27, 30, 31
alpine mummy 28-29, **29**
Ammut **23**, 30, 31
amulets 10, 11, 14, 16, **16-17**, 21, 30
Andes mummies 28
animal mummies 9, **9**, 31
anthropoid coffins 18, **18**, 21, **21**, 30
Anubis 10, 16, 20-21, **20-21**, **23**, 24, **24**, 30
Apis bulls 9, 30
Arctic mummies 28

B
ba 8, 30, 31
Bastet 9, 31
beeswax 12
boats 22, **22-23**, 27, **27**
bog people 29, **29**
Book of the Dead 16, 20, 22, 30, 31

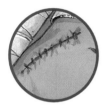

C
canopic chest 20, **21**
canopic jars 10, **10**, **18**, 20
Carnarvon, Lord 31
Carter, Howard 24, 31
coffins 18-19, **18-19**, 20-21, 22, 30
Coffin Texts 31

D
deshret 6, 31
djed-pillar 16, **16**, 30

E
Egypt 6-7, 8, 10, 14, 18, 22, 27, 30
embalming 10, 12, 14
European mummies 29, **29**
eyes 12, 18, 30

F
feather of truth 16, 23, 31
finger and toe stalls 14, **14**
funerals 22-23, 30

G
gods 6, 16, 23, 30
Greenland mummies 28, **28**

H
heart scarab 16, **16**

I
Inca mummies 28, **28**, 31
internal organs 10, 20
Inundation 6

K
ka 8, 30, 31
kemet 6
kings 7, 14, 30

L
Lindow Man 29, **29**
linen 10, 12, 14, **14**, 15, **16-17**, 31

M
Ma'at 23, **23**, 30
malachite 6, 30
masks 10, 11, 18, **18**, 19, 21, **21**, 31
mastaba 8, **8**
mourners 22, **22-23**, 30

N
natron 10, **10**, 12, 30
Nazca mummies 28
Nile 6, 22, 23

O
offerings 27, **27**, 30
oils 12, 15
Opening-of-the-Mouth ceremony 23, **23**
Osiris 16, 23, 30

P
Peruvian mummies 28, 31
pharaohs 7, **7**, 11, 30
pottery plaque 12, 30
priests 10, 14, 18, 20-21, 22
pyramids 8, **8-9**

R
resin 12, 14, **14**, 15, 18, 30

S
sarcophagus 18, 21, **21**, 22, 24, 30
shabti figures 22, 27, **27**, 30
shrines **21**, 22, 24
spells 10, 14, 16, 18, 22, 30, 31

T
Thoth 16, **16**, 23, **23**, 30
Tollund Man 29, **29**
tombs 6, 8, **8**, 21, 22, 24-25, **25**, **26-27**, 30, 31
Tutankhamun 14, 18, 21, 24, 30, 31

U
tyet-knot 16, **17**, 30

U
underworld 10, 16, 23, 27, 30
uraeus 18, **18**, 30

W
wrapping a mummy **16**, 17, **17**